the old Howe of Fife

Guthrie Hutton

The self-styled 'King o' the Common', Robert Dunn, or R. D. as he preferred to call himself, was an Auchtermuchty character of the early twentieth century. Like his father W. D., he was a mason, but when he wasn't working with stone he was out roaming the wild countryside with his little dog, gun at the ready.

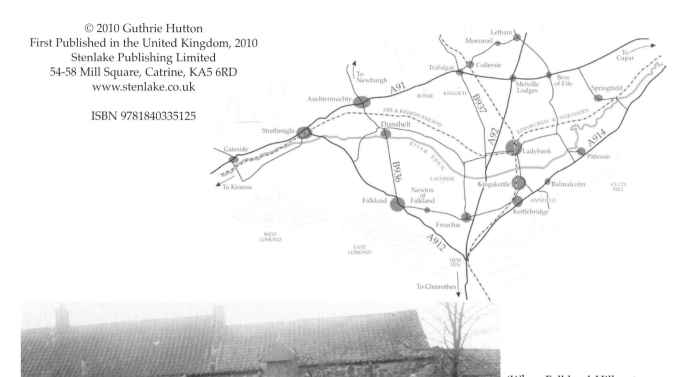

'When Falkland Hill puts on his cap, the Howe of Fife will get a drap' (variation on an old saying).

On 28th February 1925 the supply from the Freuchie Water Company's new reservoir at Denside, near the Falkland Road Station, was turned on. The ceremony was performed by Major John Lumsden, fourth from the left in the front row of this picture of the directors and their associates. He was presented with an inscribed silver cup as a memento of the occasion.

Acknowledgements

My friend and colleague Bill Fiet provided most of the pictures for this book and a lot of information. I am indebted to him and to his wife Wilma for putting up with us as we sorted through material. The representatives of the late David Anderson of Strathmiglo provided some gems, as did Eric Eunson, Elder Garland, Lynne Dunbavin, The Singing Kettle and Bernard Rodger, whose help was received for an earlier book. I am grateful also to Cupar Heritage, Cupar's local history society, for access to their collection. All over the Howe people stopped to ask if I needed help as I wandered around looking lost while trying to identify pictures and I must thank them for their kindness. A big thank you is also due to the staff at Cupar Library who were unfailingly helpful as I delved into their excellent resources searching for details.

Further Reading

Burgess, Yvonne, (compiler), *Maistly 'Muchty Memories*, 2000.

Dunbar, John G., *The Historic Architecture of Scotland*, 1966.

Falkland Society, *A Falkland Guide*, 1988.

Gifford, John, *Buildings of Scotland: Fife*, 1988.

Lamont-Brown, Raymond, *Discovering Fife*, 1988.

Lamont-Brown, Raymond, *Villages of Fife*, 2002.

McInnes, Dennis, & Richardson, Douglas, *The Changing Face of Kettle*, 1994.

Marshall, James Scott, *Freuchie Through The Years*, 1998.

Pride, Glen L., *The Kingdom of Fife, An Illustrated Architectural Guide*, 1990.

Robertson, Mairi, (Editor), *The Concise Scots Dictionary*, 1985.

Silver, Owen, *The Roads of Fife*, 1987.

Strathmiglo Primary School, *Strathmiglo Village History Walkabouts*, 1987.

Walker, Reverend George W., *Church and Parish*, 1925.

Introduction

According to *The Concise Scots Dictionary* a howe is 'a stretch of country of basin formation, a wide plain bounded by hills'. It is a definition that describes the Howe of Fife perfectly with the low-lying ground cradled by the Ochil Hills in the north, the Lomond Hills to the south west, and to the south east the high ground known as the 'Riggin o' Fife'. The basin was originally a boggy wetland, dotted with one large loch and some small ones, and through it all flowed the sluggish, ill-defined, flood-prone River Eden. With so much water in the middle, the communities of the Howe, many owing their origins to the pre-Reformation Catholic Church, clung to the better-drained higher ground around the edge of the basin.

Heath and forest clothed the drier peripheral ground and it was this that attracted Scotland's Royal family, the Stuarts, to establish their country retreat at Falkland. From their palace they could ride out into the forest and pursue the abundant game. King James V also liked to don humble clothing and as 'the guid man of Ballengeich' wander around the Howe talking to his subjects, to hear what they were thinking. The kings and their courts were accompanied by servants, soldiers and advisers and they all had to find somewhere to live. Masons and workmen who came to build the great palace had to live somewhere too, so villages other than Falkland felt the benefit of the royal presence. Some of the Stuart monarchs' favoured advisers received grants of land which over time developed into great estates, so the royal influence shaped the Howe in many ways.

The kings and courtiers had moved to London long before some of the owners of the big estates started a process of draining the lochs and bogs. The Eden was confined within high, straight banks and deep ditches were dug to drain Rossie Loch into the river channel. The loss of the wetlands would probably have troubled present day environmentalists, but the measures worked, the Howe dried out and a huge acreage of prime agricultural land was reclaimed.

Mills, maltings and other manufacturing processes were established beside the Eden and its tributary burns to deal with produce from the expanding farms. In the villages the rhythmic clatter of hand looms could be heard from most of the little cottages as people worked long hours in an attempt to earn their living by weaving a variety of linen cloths. It was a way of life that disappeared steadily through the latter half of the nineteenth century as large factories equipped with powered looms were set up in all the villages of the Howe. The products that they made differed from one factory to another, one village to another, but for the hand loom weavers, wherever they stayed, the result was always the same.

While the transition from hand-crafted goods to machine made products was going on, the face of the Howe was also changing. Roads, which had previously avoided the boggy expanse, were driven straight across it, quickly followed by railways and with them came the creation of an entirely new town, Ladybank.

Through the twentieth century the power loom factories gradually closed and the people of the Howe had to find new ways to earn a living. Farming and associated industries assumed greater importance. In the age of the motor car the Howe's proximity to larger towns and cities provided an opportunity for commuter living, new housing developments, farm shops and garden centres. Forest walks and other attractions proved popular with local people, while in the season tourists from further afield started to pour into the area to admire the places royalty left behind. Although the Stuarts departed at the start of the seventeenth century, their legacy is still contributing to the prosperity of the Howe in the twenty-first.

The broad basin of the Howe of Fife is framed by the Lomond Hills in this view looking west from the road over the Garlie Bank.

Gateside, the western gateway to the Howe, was for a time served by rail as well as road. The Fife & Kinross Railway was opened in three sections, from Ladybank to Strathmiglo in 1857, through Gateside to Milnathort in March 1858 and to Kinross in August of that year. With access to markets both to the east and west, Gateside was well-placed for the movement of agricultural produce and later for moving sugar beet to the factory at Cupar. Industry in the shape of the Gateside Mill also thrived with good rail connections, especially after the opening of the Forth Bridge in 1890. The station is seen here about 1903.

As it nears the sea, the Eden is a broad, strong river, quite unlike the modest stream dammed by this mill sluice. The scene in this picture captivated the person who used it as a postcard: 'a charming spot close to the railway embankment' they wrote 'where white marguerites are in full flower'. What they didn't say was that behind them was the Gateside Mill which made bobbins for the textile industries. The mill was the mainstay of the village and remained so despite a fire in 1874 that destroyed the main part of the buildings and another that did extensive damage in 1939. The mill had stopped using water power long before that time, and diversified into making furniture before closing and being turned into a small business estate.

Gateside Post Office, which also doubled as the village shop, is seen here in the 1930s with the shopkeeper, clad in jacket, tie and apron, posing for the photograph with the Brooke Bond Tea van driver. At the time Gateside consisted of only 23 houses, a figure that more than doubled when 30 council houses were built at Bower Park, but even with the increased population the shop eventually had to close.

Formerly known as Edenshead and with land in the area owned by the monks of Balmerino Abbey, Gateside is an old settlement site. It even has an 'old town', a delightful enclave virtually hidden from the modern A91 road, but on a loop of what was once the main road. Outwardly little has changed from this view, although the eighteenth century smithy in the foreground has been converted into a house.

Building a memorial hall, to honour the men who had died during the First World War, was a big commitment for a small community, but Gateside had needed such a facility for a long time, so people responded positively to the idea. Brigadier General G. R. H. Cheape of Wellfield gifted the site and local mill owner, Mr G. C. Leburn, helped financially and the hall was ready for its opening on 29th October 1921. After the ceremony, performed by General Douglas Campbell, Mrs Cheape unlocked the door with a silver key and a sale of work was held to augment hall funds.

Edenshead Church, on the left of the upper picture, is on the right of this one taken about 1910. It also contained a war memorial, two stained glass windows designed by A. Ballantyne & Son of Edinburgh and installed either side of the pulpit by Mr and Mrs Thom of Nether Pitlochie. One window honoured their son, Captain J. Flockhart Thom MC of the Fife & Forfar Yeomanry, who died a few weeks before the end of the war. The other window, intended as a posthumous gift from Captain Thom, honoured the other Gateside men who had been killed. Edenshead Church was originally a United Secession Church erected in 1823. Reunited with the Church of Scotland in 1929, it closed in 2007 when the congregation amalgamated with the parish church in Strathmiglo.

Originally a simple laird's house dating from 1740, the central part of Wellfield House was extended in 1800 with the addition of the east and west wings. It was the latter that fell victim to a fire in December 1929 caused by an electrical fault. Brigadier General Cheape and his wife must have been relieved that the blaze was contained to the one wing, but it seems likely that a spark was smouldering in a hidden corner of the old house, because a couple of days later flames burst out again. The main part of the house was destroyed along with many of the contents. The east wing also suffered from water damage.

Pitlour House, to the north of Strathmiglo, is a fine Georgian mansion designed by the architect Robert Mylne and built in 1783/84 for Colonel Philip Skene. The Skene family played a big role in Strathmiglo life and Pitlour, like all the great houses in the Howe, provided a significant amount of employment for local people in the form of domestic service, tending the gardens or working on the estates.

The Strathmiglo name is a conundrum. The Strath bit is easy (it means a broad river valley), but the Miglo River does not appear on modern maps because it is an old name for the upper reaches of the Eden. The village name did feature on a railway station, opened on the north side of the village in June 1857. It operated for almost a century before the growth of road transport spelled the end for passenger services in June 1950. Goods traffic continued until October 1964, but only one villager went to see the historic departure of the last train.

The west end of High Street is seen here looking east with the thatched cottage on the left situated at the junction with Station Road. Originally a single storey house, the dormer window was added early in the twentieth century and the whole building had been replaced by a two storey structure by the mid 1930s. The trees on the right hand edge of the picture indicate the site of the West Church.

A congregation of the Reformed Presbyterian Church was formed in Strathmiglo in 1823, but did not have a dedicated place of worship until 1852. It was called the North Church after the union of the Reformed Presbyterian and Free Churches in 1876 and after further church unions became known as the West Church. It had ceased to be used for regular services by 1935 when, just after midnight one January morning, it went up in flames which gutted the building and severely damaged the roof of the church hall in the foreground of this picture. Firemen also had to save a house fifty yards away when wind borne sparks ignited its roof, and threatened other buildings. After the fire the church was rebuilt as a hall and, with the roof clad in asbestos sheeting, it became known locally as the asbestos church.

The River Eden was harnessed at numerous points along its length to provide power for mills. Many of these were set on higher ground so that they were in less danger of being flooded. This meant that the lades feeding the water to them were often quite long and served more than one mill. The weir running across the foreground of this picture is directing water through the sluice on the right and into a lade that fed both the Strathmiglo bleachfield and the East Mill which ground meal and barley. The West Mill, out of picture to the left, also ground meal, and worked off the tail race of the Corston Mill, further west. Strathmiglo Primary School can be seen through the trees in the left background.

Strathmiglo's wonderfully distinctive town house steeple, seen on the front cover and in this view looking east along High Street, was erected in 1734 using stones from a building known as Strathmiglo Castle. It had been hastily erected by Sir William Scott of Balwearie in an attempt to impress King James V, but the king was scornful and the unsound structure was in a ruinous state when the good folk of Strathmiglo were looking for stones to build their tower. In front of it is the shop of A. T. Hogg whose boots and country wear business, started in 1888, helped to spread Strathmiglo's name around the world. The slightly less famous furniture warehouse of W. P. Ford, erected in 1905, is on the left.

The town house steeple is also prominent in this view of High Street looking west about 1910. The town house was the centre of civic life in the village and the stair that can be seen rising to first floor level gave access to the main part of the building, bypassing the cells that occupied the base of the tower. In the street a horse-hauled carriage and an early motor car reflect the transition from one form of transport to the other. On the right, beyond the house with the porch and railings, is George Smith's baker's shop and tea room.

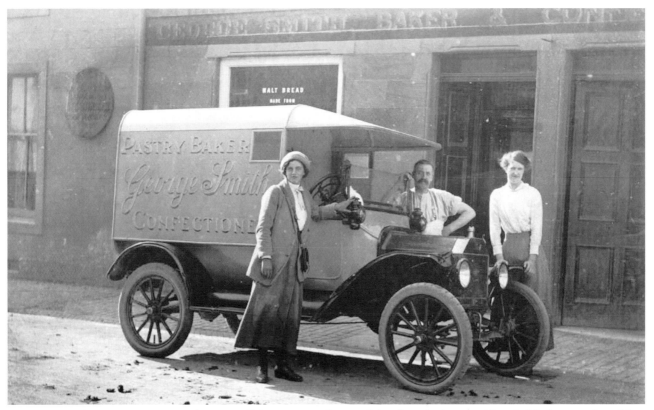

Baker and confectioner, George Smith, was well-known in and around Strathmiglo, but would probably have preferred less publicity in March 1918 when he and his van driver Magdalene Terras appeared at Cupar Sheriff Court. They were charged with offering twenty loaves for sale, baked more than twelve hours previously. The bread had gone out on Magdalene's van before the error was discovered and although she was stopped, one loaf had been sold. Smith was ordered to pay a ten shilling fine or go to jail for five days. Magdalene was admonished. Although the date of this picture and the identity of the people is not known, it is tempting to believe that the van driver could be Magdalene, with George and another woman behind.

Most modern traffic on the A91 road scoots past Strathmiglo on a bypass built in the 1970s to ease congestion in the village, although parked cars and High Street's uneven line and width continue to present a challenge to buses and delivery vans. Such problems would have been unimaginable to the two wee boys standing at the east end of the street in this picture from about 1910. Kirk Wynd runs off to the right, just beyond the buildings on the right which, like some others in the picture have been replaced.

Before the Reformation of 1560 a Catholic church dedicated to St Martin gave the village its early name of Eglismartin. It stood on a site where Strathmiglo Parish Church was built in 1783/84. It is probable that a Protestant church occupied the site in the period between these two churches and an inscribed stone, thought to come from it and dated 1647, is incorporated above the entrance. It was erected in 1938 to replace the vestry and Session House. This early twentieth century view from the adjacent 'God's acre' has been altered by that new entrance and other changes that include an increase in the number of graves and size of the trees.

Creating a bowling green in Strathmiglo was a community effort. A company of local people drove the project and raised the necessary funds. The site and annual rent was donated by Mr W. B. Skene of Pitlour. Mr R. D. Thom of Nether Pitlochie gifted the turf - regarded as the best in the district - and neighbouring farmers did the carting free of charge. Favoured by such goodwill, the green was ready for its opening in July 1901. Mr Skene threw the first bowl and this was followed by a match between Strathmiglo and a team of visitors from neighbouring clubs. Strath won. Since those early days the pavilion has been considerably enlarged and some of the buildings in the background have gone.

Strathmiglo Market-Games

Held on the first Saturday in July and continuing a long tradition, the Strathmiglo Market-Games was a big event for a small village. As times changed, so did some of the events, with competitions for dancing, fancy dress and tug-o-war held before the Second World War being omitted from this programme for 1955. At the heart of the games were races for runners over distances ranging from 100 yards to two miles. Competitors were given a handicapped start and cash prizes were awarded for all events. Two wrestling competitions were held and heavy events included throwing the weight, putting the shot and tossing the caber. There were cycle races on bikes that had no gears and no brakes, so it was a real test of strength and skill to maintain speed and traction round the grass track. The highlight was the one mile cycle race for the coveted Lomond Trophy, with no handicaps and all competitors starting from scratch. Side-shows and amusements were all part of the fun and after their exertions, villagers and competitors could unwind at the Grand Games-Night Dance in the town hall. The King George V Playing Field, where the games were held, is seen beyond the children's play park in the picture taken about the 1950s.

Known as the Chrysanthemum Concert Party, these exotically dressed performers were photographed in 1918 and probably took part in one of the events staged every day of a week in July that year to raise funds for the Red Cross. There was a sale of work, an evening of sacred music, a concert by schoolchildren at Gateside and a host of other entertainments that together earned the unexpectedly high sum of £400.

Strathmiglo is split by the River Eden with the old part of the village to the north and the newer thoroughfares of Skene Street and Cash Feus to the south. This was the industrial part of the village as can be seen in this view looking north from the high ground overlooking Skene Street. This was a street of weavers, working either at looms in their own cottages or as employees of A. N. Thomson's Skene Works. The prominent factory chimney shows that it was the hand loom weaver's worst nightmare, a power loom works driven by steam, not water power.

With cliff-like buildings and an arrow-straight road, the architecture of Skene Street is much more industrial looking than anything else in this part of Fife. The Skene Works, on the right of this picture looking west along Skene Street, was kept busy meeting Government contracts for a variety of cloths during the First World War and contributing to the export drive after the Second, but the unfavourable conditions that followed caused its closure in 1963. The East Bank Linen Works, off Cash Feus, had closed a few years earlier in 1958.

Cash Feus was another street of weavers' cottages that was named after the Cash Estate from which the ground was feued. When he heard about the name it got the American folk singer Johnny Cash to thinking that it could be where his family had originated. Right or wrong he would probably have felt some kinship with these children, from humble origins like his own, playing in the street in the 1950s.

Little girls wearing linen smocks dutifully pose for this picture of Cash Feus taken about 1905. A feu was a piece of land granted as heritable property by a landowner for another person's exclusive use in return for payment. In feudal times, where the term originated, this could be in the form of military service or grain, but later it was in money. From 1974 it was possible for people to buy out their feus and no new feu contracts could be imposed. Prior to that, feuing was often used to provide land to expand communities and for some, like Cash Feus, this did not just include the housing plots, but also what was essentially a private road with public access. With so many people sharing an expense that few could afford the road was inevitably poorly maintained until it was taken over by the local authority.

Private carriages have pulled to the side and a small crowd of people has gathered to watch this troop of mounted soldiers walk westward along Auchtermuchty's Low Road. Their actual identity is not known, but they could be men of the Fife & Forfar Yeomanry. The picture was taken around the time of the South African, or Boer, War, a conflict for which the locally recruited light cavalry regiment, was well-suited, and where it served with distinction.

The findings of a Royal Commission, set up in 1912, were incorporated into the Housing Act of 1919, the first of a number of acts that gave local authorities powers to clear old substandard dwellings and build new homes. Auchtermuchty Town Council withdrew from an early plan to erect houses at Mournipae, but in the early 1930s, having looked at a number of locations, decided to build on a site to the south of Low Road. Known as Stratheden Place, the scheme was designed by architects, Gillespie & Scott of St Andrews, and the first tenants were approved in March 1933. More houses were built over the next few years.

Despite major alterations to the cottages, this view from about 1900, looking east along High Road, is still recognisable. Perhaps the most obvious change is that the roofs are no longer thatched. Once common throughout the Howe, thatch was a particular feature of Auchtermuchty. With reeds obtained from Lindores Loch or the fringes of the Tay, it continued as a roofing material well into the twentieth century, aided by a local council that took a benign view of official attempts to limit its use.

The former Bank of Scotland building is on the left of this view of High Street looking toward the old market place, where the Mercat (market) Cross once stood. It was a symbol of Auchtermuchty's Royal Burgh status, granted in 1517. In the 1860s a drinking fountain was donated to the town and erected on the site in front of the Commercial Hotel, but it had no water supply or gas for the light, so people bumped into it in the dark and it came to be regarded as an embarrassing nuisance. It was removed about 1880 and the place where it stood was later used for the war memorial. The hotel, an early nineteenth century coaching inn, has in its time also been named the Boar's Head and Forest Hills Hotel.

The Auchtermuchty Co-operative Society store is on the right of this early twentieth century view of High Street. Before coming together as a single entity, five separate co-operative societies operated in the town. Hand loom weavers had their own linen manufacturers society which fizzled out with the demise of their trade, but there was also a baking society and others selling groceries and clothing, boots and shoes, and coal. The shop seen here later became the Tannochbrae Tearoom, a reflection of the time when the town was used as the location for the Scottish Television drama series, Doctor Finlay's Casebook.

William Stocks took over an established bookshop on the corner of Croft and Kirk Wynd - the old name of High Street - and later moved into the shop seen here which had formerly been a drapery. Early in his career he became the town's postmaster, and continued as that throughout his working life. In his other role as a bookseller and stationer he sold picture postcards, some of which may appear in this book.

A line-up of smartly dressed senior citizens is seen here in front of the post office in a picture entitled 'Pension Day'. It was used as a postcard in 1909, and this, combined with the subject matter, suggests that the people could be Auchtermuchty's first state pensioners. Introduced in 1908, the old age pension was a means tested, non-contributory scheme that paid a maximum of five shillings a week to people over 70 years of age, and recipients were excluded from poor relief.

It had been a wet spring in 1916 followed by more heavy rain in early summer. The ground was saturated and water levels were high when torrential rain started to fall late on the evening of Thursday 6th July. It lasted through the following day and was still pouring on the Saturday morning when residents of the Greens and Burnside woke to the sound of water filling their houses. The burn had been overwhelmed by water cascading off the hills and to this was added an angry brown torrent pouring down the Abernethy Road at an alarming speed and depth. Men broke gaps in the Burnside walls to relieve the pressure, but it made no difference as the flood deepened to several feet, cutting the village in two. People living near the distillery had to be rescued through the windows of their flooded homes. The meal and saw mills were both inundated and the bleachfield was badly damaged. The railway was awash and train services were curtailed when the Barroway Burn undermined the track to Strathmiglo. Between them the overflowing burns flooded all the ground to Dunshelt and it was a similar story across the Howe where the words 'never seen anything like it' were on everyone's lips and for once, were entirely accurate.

Although it caused mayhem in 1916 the burn was central to life in Auchtermuchty; physically because it divided the town and economically because it provided work and wealth. It even impressed King James V who boasted that its little stone bridges were finer than any over the Thames, ignoring the obvious differences of scale and distance, but that's probably the prerogative of kings. The lower, southern end of Burnside is seen here in a picture from the late 1930s or early 1940s.

Higher up the burn, but still looking south, the meal mill can be seen on the right of this picture with, on the extreme right, a wooden trough-like lade which would have been used to feed water to the mill wheel. The modern housing of Burnside Court has been built where this lade once flowed. The thatched building in the left foreground has also disappeared.

One of the little bridges that James V boasted about spans the burn in this view looking north. Just poking into the picture on the left is one of the industries that made use of the burn, Alexander Bonthrone's Stratheden Distillery. Its closure in the 1920s, after more than a century of operation, was a blow to the town: the demolition of the buildings dismayed many people.

This tranquil picture looking south at the Upper Greens offers a stark contrast with the upper picture of the 1916 flood on page 23. It is scarcely believable that they show the same burn, but they do! The modern motor age has intruded into this scene with a small car park occupying the space where the children are standing. Another small car park, close to the distant trees, lets visitors stop and admire the statue of Auchtermuchty's favourite son, accordionist, band leader and all round icon of Scottishness, Jimmy Shand.

Like Washington, Auchtermuchty has a White House. It occupies a prominent site at the gushet between Mournipae on the left and Newburgh Road and would at one time have almost been surrounded by the linen trade. There were weavers' cottages in Mournipae and the factory chimney on the right was at Lambert's Works. Arnott's Works, from which Arnott Street takes its name, was further down the burn. These power loom factories had closed by the 1930s, unable to survive the massive rise in the cost of raw materials and imports of cheap cotton goods.

To the north of the town was the Skinner family's bleachfield where linen yarn was treated and whitened before going to the mills to be woven into cloth. Located beside the Newburgh road and the burn, its buildings, machinery and stock were badly affected by the flood of 1916. With its fortunes closely tied to those of the linen factories, it stopped working when they did in the slump in trade that followed the First World War.

Auchtermuchty's nine hole golf course was opened in 1903. It commanded splendid views from its hillside location behind the town, although the fifth hole, seen here, was perhaps not its most scenic. The picture was used as a postcard by someone named Stocks, who identified the two men on the right as the Reverend Affleck and 'Willie' - possibly William Stocks, the postmaster. The course was ploughed up in 1943 as part of the wartime drive to 'dig for victory'.

A 36 yard square bowling green, sufficient for five rinks, was laid out on the site of an old quarry at the head of the town. Plans and specifications had been prepared by a Mr Speirs of Newburgh Bowling Club and members of that club were present when Provost White opened the green in early June 1890. They and the members of the new club spent an enjoyable evening inaugurating the new green.

In 1733 a group of churchmen gathered at Gairney Bridge near Kinross to declare their independence from the Church of Scotland. They disliked the compromises that the church had to make to conform to its established status, and the way a minister could be imposed on a congregation by a powerful patron. Born out of a spirit of dissent, the Secession Church that they founded was prone to squabbling and spawned a number of branches before these came together again in 1847 as the United Presbyterian Church. With a strong secessionist streak, Auchtermuchty had three such churches, later reduced to two, the South U.P. and North U.P. Churches. The latter is seen here with an inset showing the Reverend John Morison who was minister in the early twentieth century. The North Church was later used as an Episcopal Church.

The issues that caused the secession of 1733 festered inside the Church of Scotland for over a century until they burst into the open in 1843 in an event known as the Disruption. Almost half of all ministers and their congregations left the established church to form the Free Church of Scotland. Within a few years new churches appeared all over Scotland including one in Auchtermuchty; the Martyrs Church. It became a United Free Church in 1900 when the United Presbyterian and Free Churches amalgamated. It is seen here shortly after that event with an inset of its minister the Reverend William Affleck. The Martyrs and South United Free Churches amalgamated in 1923, six years before the full reunion of the United Free Church and Church of Scotland.

With much of the country's social provision based on parish structures, the impact of church divisions was felt beyond the world of religious affairs. Often there were two or three church-based parish schools in an area until the Education Act of 1872 placed such provision in the hands of School Boards, and made it compulsory for all children between the ages of five and thirteen to attend. The Boards either built a new school or took over an existing building, like the one in Auchtermuchty adjacent to the North Church. It was upgraded and enlarged in 1905.

These 'little soldiers' formed part of the Auchtermuchty Parish Church Junior Choir that gave a concert in the Victoria Hall in May 1915. They performed war, Gipsy and other songs in an an effort to raise funds for destitute Belgian children and to provide Bovril for the troops. They gave a repeat performance later in the week for the Serbian Relief Fund.

The Auchtermuchty Band was an institution, playing not just in the town, but at functions throughout the Howe. The bandsmen are seen here about 1905, boarding a charabanc at the Royal Hotel to set off for another engagement. The mid- nineteenth century hotel on the Cupar Road was, as the picture shows, a place where travellers could stable their horses or hire a post-chaise.

In the 1920s, when this picture was taken, travellers heading east on the A91 road had to negotiate the slight hump of the bridge over the burn and then jouk through the gap between the buildings. That changed in the late 1930s when the bridge was rebuilt and some small buildings in the picture were knocked down to allow the road to be widened. On the left, facing camera but partly hidden, is the Victoria Hall which was erected in 1865 and became the centre of Auchtermuchty social life. Dances, whist drives and performances by the local drama and music groups were just some of the entertainments on offer. Twice weekly showings of movies, organised by the proprietors of the Royal Hotel, were also popular until halted by the advance of television: the projection box was later made into a bar. The large building behind the Victoria Hall was a linen factory operated by A. N. Thomson of Strathmiglo.

Across the Cupar Road from Victoria Hall, on the corner of Station Road, was John Cunnison's family grocer's shop. On the wall is a sign promoting Quaker Oats which, had it remained in place for a while, could have incorporated an arrow pointing to Uthrogle Mills outside Cupar. A former flax mill, it had been used to make Scotts Porage Oats since 1947 and was taken over by Quaker in 1982. Cunnison's shop later became 'The Corner Shop' run by Willie Masson and then an estate agent's business.

Later generations would come to regard standing in the middle of the A91 as a bit risky, but in the Edwardian era people happily complied with this photographer's request to do just that. The only wheeled vehicle in sight is a bicycle. The picture is looking west with the eighteenth century Cameron House on the left. Unusually, this historic structure has survived the advance of the modern world and it is the road that has had to make compromises.

Station Road is on the right behind these youngsters sitting on the grass, enjoying the sun. To their left, hidden from view at the base of the wall, is the burn and behind the wall is the area where two metal working businesses were located.

Some time before 1715 the firm of John White & Sons began to make weighing beams and scales. Easily the oldest manufacturer of weighing machines in the country, they encouraged the firm of Robert Ferlie to set up in the town in 1877, to make iron castings for some of their products. As time went on White's continued to make their own castings and Ferlie's diversified, so that between them, unusually for the Howe, they gave Muchty a metal moulding and light engineering industry.

The Fife & Kinross Railway opened its Auchtermuchty station in 1857. It was a single track line, so only one platform was needed to serve trains going in both directions. It could get crowded on high days, holidays and special occasions as this picture, taken early in the twentieth century, shows. At the time the line was operated by the North British Railway, but by the time the nationalised British Railways took over in 1948 such numbers had dwindled. The station was closed to passengers in June 1950 although the line remained open for freight for a few more years.

The curlers of Auchtermuchty were a bit peeved in December 1844 because they had just secured a splendid site for a pond, but had not been able to get it ready before a hard frost set in. The 50 yard square site on the Myres Estate had a good water supply and was sheltered by trees and walls which kept the water still and the ice, consequently, smooth. Playing as the Stratheden Club in the Cupar Province, the Muchty curlers often won the bonspiels that the seemingly more frequent hard winters made possible around 1905, when this picture appears to have been taken.

The Myres of Auchtermuchty, a name that implies marshy lands, were granted in the 15th century to John Scrymgeour, the King's claviger (key bearer, or macer) a title that was subsequently attached to the estate regardless of ownership. The oldest element of Myres Castle is a tower house dating from about 1540, but the most distinctive part of the structure is the two storey ashlar addition built above it in 1616 and seen in the centre of the picture. It was erected by Stephen Paterson who bought the estate in 1611. He was followed by a number of other owners who added further wings and extensions to the original structure.

The Cheape family, who acquired Rossie Estate in 1669, had a major impact on the Howe of Fife. They partially drained the Rossie Loch in 1740/41 by cutting a drain to the River Eden and then by widening and deepening the drain in 1805/06 they fully drained the loch to create a level expanse of rich farm land. Rossie House was built about 1700 as an extension to an earlier laird's house which appears to have been taken down about 1767 when the bow fronted wing, on the right, was added.

Kinloch, the name means 'at the head of the loch', has been a misnomer since the draining of Rossie Loch. The old house has also disappeared, incorporated into the structure of the mansion, erected in 1859 to the designs of the owner's brother, Charles Kinnear and modified in the 1920s by another architect, Robert Lorimer. In November 1902 a shed at Kinloch Home Farm caught fire and much of the estate's produce for the year was destroyed. The flames were fought by estate workers and firemen from Kingskettle, one of whom was injured when he fell into a disused well.

The draining of Rossie Loch and the wetlands of the Howe ultimately succeeded because the lairds of Lathrisk also dealt with the River Eden's constant floods by straightening its course and confining it within embankments. Lathrisk was the original name for Kettle Parish, and Lathrisk House is thought to have been built on the site of a pre-Reformation church. Part of that early building may have been incorporated into the mansion which was reconstructed in 1786 with the classical Georgian facade seen in this picture.

The little village of Dunshelt is 137 feet above sea level on the road between Auchtermuchty and Falkland. It is seen here looking south along Main Street in the late 1930s or early 1940s. Traffic has increased since then, but here there is only one car and it is being driven on the wrong side of the road, presumably not because Fifers can be a law unto themselves, but because a photographer was in the way.

A little further south along Dunshelt Main Street and another photographer has taken up a position in the middle of the road to take this view of the post office, with a small group of villagers outside. Main Street's junction with the Wynd is on the left, behind the building in the foreground which was used as branch of the Auchtermuchty Co-op.

When something technical was wrong in the early days of television a caption appeared on the screen advising viewers not to adjust their sets. A similar warning should probably accompany these two pictures, because while both are good images they are sadly blurred. They look north along the same bit of Main Street as in the lower picture on the facing page, but instead of parked cars, these pictures show the smithy of Alexander Duncan & Son. In common with many village blacksmiths they turned their skills to mending motor vehicles when these were introduced and over time their workshops morphed into garages. The white painted building facing camera on the right is the Co-op on the corner of the Wynd.

This closer view of the smithy shows it with an assortment of agricultural equipment outside. Making and repairing such machinery was traditionally the main source of employment for a country blacksmith, but here it provides a contrasting background to the group of little girls dressed in their Edwardian finery.

A little human drama seems to have unfolded here. A photographer has lined up a picture looking out along Ladybank Road with a man walking away from camera and another cycling toward it. At the critical moment a girl has stepped out from Regent Terrace and, in a classic gesture of someone who thinks they may have intruded, has put her hand to her mouth. Oops!

The southern end of Main Street is seen here looking south, with the building opened in 1841 as the Dunshelt Improvement Society School in the left foreground. Otherwise most of the buildings in this and the other pictures of Dunshelt were formerly weavers' cottages. In the first half of the nineteenth century the weavers were fully occupied and the village was prosperous. Every house was occupied, but when linen factories were set up in the surrounding towns and villages, people began to move out and look for work elsewhere. The trend was halted when a power loom works was set up at the north end of the village in the 1870s.

What's in a name? Dunshelt has been defined as either Danes-halt, the place where defeated Danes stopped after fleeing from a battle on Falkland Moor, or as 'the fort by the river', a dun being a fort or fortified hill. It is of course possible that neither theory is correct, but, whatever the name, the village would be just the same. It is seen here looking north from the bridge over the River Eden.

There can be little doubt that the two pictures on this page were taken within a few minutes of each other because the same people appear in each one, notably the woman and child on the left of this picture who can be seen in the centre of the upper picture, wearing the same clothes. The picture is entitled Dunshelt Harbour and although such a facility might seem unlikely, many miles from the sea on a river spanned by numerous weirs, stories exist of boats being used, either for eel fishing, or carrying light goods on the clear, canalised, middle section across the Howe.

Falkland Castle originally belonged to the MacDuffs, the Earls of Fife, and when their line died out it passed to the Earl of Mentieth, Robert Stuart, who later became the Duke of Albany. While acting as Regent of Scotland he brought his nephew, David Stuart, Duke of Rothesay and heir to the throne, to Falkland where, under mysterious circumstances, the young man died in 1402. The truth of what happened will never be known, but Falkland Castle will forever be tainted with the suspicion that a murder most foul was committed within its walls. David's younger brother eventually became King James I, but until that happened Albany remained as Regent. He died in 1420 and his son Murdoch, the Second Duke, was executed a few years later. Falkland passed to his great uncle Walter Stuart, Earl of Atholl, who was tortured to death in 1437 for his part in the assassination of James I. Falkland was forfeited to the Crown and James II began the process of extending and enhancing what was now a Royal Palace. Starting about 1458, he added a Great Hall adjacent to the old castle, but time and a fire in 1654 when Cromwell's troops were billeted in the hall have taken their toll and only some foundations of both castle and hall remain.

The most distinctive part of Falkland Palace is the fortified gatehouse completed in 1541, although apart from an incident in 1592 when the Earl of Bothwell tried to force an entry, the Stuart monarchs were probably more at risk from enemies within the Palace than without. To the right of the gatehouse is the south range of buildings erected about 1511-1513 by James IV.

With James VI moving to London after the Union of the Crowns in 1603 royal visits to Falkland dwindled. Almost 200 years had passed since the last one when, in 1820, a Professor John Bruce bought both the Myres Estate at Auchtermuchty and Nuthill Estate at Falkland, which included what was still a Royal Palace. On his death, his niece Margaret Bruce inherited the estates and this very wealthy woman married an Eton and Oxford educated barrister, Onesiphorous Tyndall, who added Bruce to his own name. The Tyndall-Bruces were beneficent landowners who took estate management and duties of care seriously, including providing such things as the Bruce Fountain, which gave the village a reliable source of wholesome water. It was completed in 1856, the year after Onesiphorous died, and is seen here with two boys, one clothed as a lowland toff, the other in highland garb. They seem sullen and resentful, perhaps acting out Scotland's age-old antipathies, or maybe they were just fed up with the photographer who had asked them to dress up.

Nuthill House, about a mile to the west of Falkland was for a while the Tyndall-Bruce's home, but preferring something grander they had it demolished and commissioned the architect William Burn to design a new home. Erected between 1839 and 1844, Falkland House was a large and imposing mansion set in extensive landscaped gardens. Having outlived her husband, Margaret Tyndall-Bruce died childless in 1869 and the estate passed to a relative whose son sold it in 1887 to John, third Marquis of Bute, a man with impeccable Stuart ancestry.

As Hereditary Constable, Captain and Keeper of the Palace the Marquis of Bute began to carry out work to preserve its fabric and restore the south range, making it habitable again. The only part of the Palace where the interior had survived was the Chapel Royal with its 1540s period timber panelling and screen. It was in urgent need of attention to prevent its demise and the work of preservation and restoration was started by the Marquis and carried on by his successors.

Scotland's turbulent history of feuds, warring factions and murderous plots has left the country with a legacy of ruined structures shorn of their former glory. One such ruin is the surviving fragment of the east range, seen here on the right. Built in the time of King James IV, both it and the south range were embellished with buttresses and carved stone medallions made by French master masons brought in by James V in 1537-41. The quality of the exterior, arguably the finest early Renaissance architecture in Britain, makes the loss of the interior, and the rest of the structure, doubly sad. The memorial to the Bruce family, on the left, was a somewhat intrusive addition that has since been removed.

Visitors, like this group photographed in front of the Bruce Memorial, have long been drawn to Falkland to gaze on its splendours. In order to make these available to as many people as possible, and ensure that the work of restoration and presentation continued to a high standard, the National Trust for Scotland was appointed Deputy Keeper in 1952. Since then the palace and garden have attracted numerous visitors to Falkland, with undoubted benefits for the local community, many of whom act as volunteers for the Trust.

Mrs J. Hardie's Temperance Hotel occupied a building directly across the road from the palace gatehouse. It was next door to two very fine seventeenth century houses, one of which is Moncrief House. It dates from 1610 and still shelters under the last thatched roof in Falkland. Its gable is on the right of the picture, adjacent to the hotel.

With a backdrop of East Lomond, this view over Falkland from the upper works of the Palace, has as its principal focus the town hall, built in 1800/01. This was where the town council met before local government reorganisation in 1975 created North East Fife District Council, which itself was superseded by the single tier Fife Council twenty years later. The National Trust for Scotland acquired the building in 1986 to provide exhibition space, and a reception place for visiting parties. The parish church spire is on the right.

A new parish church was built in Falkland in 1620 and, from contemporary descriptions, it sounds like a typical old Scots preaching box with a bellcote topping one of the gable ends. A door in the east end gave access to an aisle along the north side. There were galleries, but at 28 feet wide it must have been a squash to seat the many hundreds of people who were apparently able to get in. Repaired in 1772 it was still dilapidated inside with an earth floor and decayed seats. Small wonder then, that what sounds like an ecclesiastical slum, was knocked down and replaced in 1849-1850 by a new church designed by the architect David Bryce and paid for by Onesiphorous Tyndall Bruce.

With what sounds like a thoroughly uncomfortable place of worship, parishioners who were tempted to support the Disruption of 1843 would have an added reason to walk out of the Established Church of Scotland. They erected a new Free Church building in 1844 which must have riled those remaining with the old church until their rich patron came to the rescue five years later. The Free Church building became the church hall after reunification of the churches in 1929.

The tall house on the left of this picture looking west from the Cross is believed to be where Richard Cameron, a significant figure in Scotland's religious history, was born in 1648. Originally a school teacher, his presbyterian views hardened against the attempts by King Charles II to impose Episcopacy in Scotland. He became known as the Lion of the Covenant, prepared to fight to defend what he regarded as religious and civil liberty. And fight he did in July 1680 when confronted by a party of dragoons on Airds Moss in Ayrshire. He was killed along with eight of his companions and his head carried triumphantly into Edinburgh on the end of a pike.

In the centre of this view looking toward the West Port is the Weaver's Cottage, in reality two cottages made into one. The restoration of the building, done by the National Trust for Scotland, has helped to preserve the memory of a trade that provided a living for many townspeople in the centuries that followed the colourful royal times. The little cottages contrast sharply with Bruce's Building, on the left, erected in 1869 in the somewhat incongruous Victorian Baronial style.

The town's old burial ground contains many interesting headstones set up over the course of about 200 years from the mid seventeenth century. Its entrance can be seen in this view looking towards the centre of town from the West Port, sandwiched between the thatched cottage on the right and the tall building, with its gable set to the road.

The West Port, the western entry and exit from the town, is seen here looking west. The trees in the background screen Falkland House the occupants of which must have been familiar with these houses on their way in and out of town.

Cross Wynd takes its name from the Mercat Cross which was situated at its northern end. Falkland was granted Royal Burgh status in 1458 by King James II, a position that brought with it significant trading privileges, so a mercat cross was a symbol of a burgh's importance. Sadly, the name of Cross Wynd might equally have reflected the way people felt when the range of buildings on the right of this picture was demolished. These fine examples of Scots vernacular architecture were initially saved from demolition in 1937 by a group of people calling themselves the Friends of Falkland Society, but with the nation's finances depleted by a world war, the money to restore them could not be raised. A car park now occupies the site.

Horse Market, seen here looking toward Cross Wynd from Back Wynd, almost certainly got its name from being the location of a market that was made possible by Falkland's Royal Burgh status. On the left, indicated by the sign for P. & P. Campbell's Perth Dye Works, is a licensed grocery which, as well as groceries sold wines, spirits, confectionery and tobacco.

A stream of people, mainly young women, walks purposefully up South Street. With everyone going in the one direction they must be going somewhere, or more likely returning from either the Congregational Church further down the street, or perhaps, at the end of a shift, from the Pleasance Linen Factory on the eastern edge of town. The right hand edge of the picture is framed by Wellbrae House, a fine Scots vernacular dwelling which sports a marriage lintel dated 1663. The picture appears to have been taken from a window on the gable of the building on the left of the Horse Market picture on the facing page.

Two linen works were set up in Falkland, the Pleasance Works, which made a variety of products including sheeting, table cloths and towelling, and the St John's Works, on the right of this picture looking up Well Brae. Initially a linen works it was turned over to making floorcloth and linoleum when Charles Jackson & Son, the owners of the Pleasance Works, took it over. The women walking towards camera can be identified as mill workers by their distinctive clothing.

In November 1919, the Scottish Co-operative Wholesale Society (SCWS) took over both the Pleasance Linen Factory and the St John's Works from Charles Jackson & Son. In 1930 they decided to expand linoleum production by erecting a new factory adjacent to the St John's Works. The prospect of having a large industrial concern built in the historic burgh divided local opinion, but the SCWS went ahead despite the opposition. The factory became a major employer in the area, more than doubling the previous workforce, and was clearly welcomed by employees like these two men beside their Albion lorry.

It took over a year to excavate 40,000 tons of earth and stone from the hillside to create the foundations for the new works, giving weight to a fifty year old prophesy that 'prosperity would never come to Falkland until the East Lomond was carried down to the Lappie', the place where the spoil was dumped. The brick building with reinforced concrete floors on steel beams was largely constructed by an SCWS workforce and their workshops at Shieldhall in Glasgow supplied the office furniture. The roads around the works were laid by an Auchtermuchty contractor. A specialist Kirkcaldy engineering firm supplied the machinery which could produce 1,000 miles of linoleum a year, in a two yard width, and could also run metric sized material for the European market.

Opponents of the lino works did have a point. Sitting on an elevated site, rising to a height of 87 feet and with a chimney almost 50 feet higher, it towered over the town and imposed itself on the landscape. It is probable, however, that the great and good of the co-operative wholesale movement were not troubled by such considerations in late June 1934 as they made their way from Glasgow and Edinburgh to the new factory. Arriving in special trains at Ladybank and Falkland Road Stations, they were taken by bus to Falkland where William Gallagher, Director of the Society, performed the opening ceremony. The SCWS band from Glasgow provided music while other SCWS departments provided the catering.

By completing twenty houses in Lomond Crescent, in August 1922, Falkland had moved more quickly than most Fife communities in the drive to improve housing after the First World War. The architect of the scheme, Andrew Haxton from Leven, designed a mix of three, four and five roomed dwellings that also incorporated bathrooms, kitchens with sculleries, storage cellars and the most up-to-date arrangements for heating water and cooking.

The principal route in and out of the town to the east is the Pleasance, a name that must have an early connection to the palace (**pleasance:** a secluded enclosure, or part of a garden, especially one attached to a large house). It has changed since this picture was taken early in the twentieth century, with houses lining the roadside and obscuring this view of the palace. A desire to build more houses off the Pleasance sparked local anger when a wall was demolished in the spring of 2010.

Newton of Falkland, about two miles from Falkland on the road to Freuchie, is referred to in documents that date from the mid sixteenth century, so it's not very 'new'. These cottages, in a lane off Lathrisk Road, probably date from the nineteenth or late eighteenth century and have been so heavily modified in the twentieth as to make them almost unrecognisable from this picture taken about 1905.

Looking north from the main road, this view shows houses in and around Jubilee Crescent which, like those in the upper picture, have been substantially modified over the years. A house has also been built on the field where the girls are standing, making it a bit tricky to replicate the photograph which was taken about 1910.

Newton of Falkland was described in a gazetteer of the 1860s as 'an irregularly built, disagreeable place, inhabited principally by weavers'. Clearly unflattering, it was also a curious observation because it made no mention of the industry that gave the village distinctive buildings like the malthouse and brewery at Glen Newton.

The Glen Newton malthouse was taken over during the First World War by the firm of Alexander Bonthrone & Sons. The company was started in 1600 when the founder acquired the tenancy of a small brewery at Newton of Falkland and from there the business grew to become a substantial operation with interests across the Howe, including large maltings at Newton seen on the left of this picture. In malting, grain (usually barley) is steeped in water until it starts to germinate, thus converting the starch into sugar and this process is stopped at the desired stage by quickly drying the grain. The malted grain is then used in brewing or distilling.

Newton's former post office is on the left of this picture looking east along Main Street. Beyond it is a cottage that was replaced by the 'County Houses', built about 1933 by Fife County Council. The distinctive skyline of the maltings also appears in the background. Alexander Bonthrone & Sons became part of Distillers Company Ltd (DCL) in 1947, just three years short of their 350th anniversary. Since then large industrial plants have superseded craft-based operations like those at Newton and the buildings have been converted for housing.

This view of the east end of Newton was taken about 1905 and remarkably the photographer has managed to take a picture of the village that does not show part of a maltings. It does include a house on the right that has been replaced and mature trees that have also largely disappeared.

In the days when royalty frequented Falkland, Freuchie was the poor relation, close enough to be useful, far enough away to be out of sight. Its role as the place where servants and soldiers lodged is preserved in a variety of little phrases like 'Awa tae Freuchie and eat mice' and 'Gang tae Freuchie where the Froggies live' (French workmen, not little amphibians, although there may have been a few of them as well). The road from Newton would therefore have been trod by many people going to and from the palace on foot or horseback, activities that had ceased long before this picture was taken about 1905, when horse-hauled traffic was still in evidence. The fence in the left foreground marked the most westerly property in Freuchie.

Further into Freuchie, this 1936 view of the west end of High Street shows a prominent sign for the *Fife News*, a splendid paper in its day and an excellent source of stories and information for local historians. Its pages were filled with detailed snapshots of life in times past and your scribe has plundered many of these for this book. The paper was probably on sale at the shop that occupied the little lean-to building with a segmented roof, on the other side of the road.

The use of horses and carts to transport goods is still very much in evidence in this view from 1908, looking west along High Street from its junction with Green Tree Brae. James Lumsden's family grocery shop on the left has since become a private house.

Modern extensions to the houses have served to alter the detail, although not the overall impression of this view looking down Dykeside to High Street West. The picture was taken about 1927.

Freuchie had a reputation for being dirty and unkempt, with piles of refuse on the roads, and one mid-nineteenth century account described it as 'an irregularly built place in an ill-kept condition'. Such claims are hard to verify, but evidence that it was 'irregularly built' is borne out by these old thakit biggins (thatched buildings) which do not conform to any street line. Thought to have been in High Street (right) and Lomond Road (lower), these cottages would have appealed to the modern taste for restoration and upgrading, but damp, with beaten earth floors and a lack of proper sanitation led earlier generations to knock them down.

Lomond Road has barely changed in 100 years since this view, looking east, was photographed about 1909.

Freuchie's irregularity did not include these almost identical nineteenth century rows of cottages, The Feus (left) and Unthank (lower), which share many features despite being on opposite sides of the village. They are still broadly recognisable despite some fairly comprehensive alterations to structure and surroundings.

Many of the cottages in these pictures of the village originally accommodated not just people, but a hand-operated loom. The weavers were supplied with yarn by merchants who then also bought the woven cloth and sold it on through their warehouses in larger towns like Kirkcaldy or Dunfermline. At one time weavers could earn a tolerable living, but as the nineteenth century wore on their income slumped. Kirsteen Marshall, the last weaver in Freuchie, stopped work at her loom in 1906, about the same time that this photograph was taken and it is tempting to believe that she could be the woman in the picture.

As the nineteenth century progressed, hand loom weavers grew increasingly fearful of being superseded by factories operating powered looms, but in Freuchie this new technology proved to be less of a threat. One of the merchants who bought and sold their produce was a local man, Walter Lumsden. He died in 1847 and was succeeded by his son Thomas who continued to trade under the name of Walter Lumsden & Son, but expanded the business by setting up a power loom factory, the Eden Valley Works, in the 1850s. It is seen on the right of this picture, beyond the factory housing known as Eden Valley Row, erected in the 1870s.

The Eden Valley Works employed many villagers directly, or working on hand looms in their own cottages. It took over another factory in 1869 and when a third business failed, the works became the mainstay of the local economy, so much so that when lightning struck a ventilator on the weaving shed roof in May 1924, the whole community was affected. Large numbers of people turned out to fight the fire, with Major John Lumsden directing operations from the factory roof. Cupar's fire engine, which was normally horse-drawn, was hitched behind a lorry and, after stopping in Pitlessie to light the boiler fire, the firemen arrived at Freuchie with steam up for the pump. Using water from the factory pond they saved part of the works and offices, but the damage was considerable. Re-equipped with automatic looms, the works remained in production, but with a reduced workforce, until 1957.

Eden Valley Row is seen on the left of this picture with North Street receding into the distance on the right. Almost beautifully stark in its unadorned simplicity, it is typical of mill-workers' housing erected throughout nineteenth century Britain, and a striking contrast to old Freuchie's more random townscape.

A different kind of contrast existed between the mill workers housing of North Street and Eden Valley House, the Lumsden family home. An elaborate letter 'L' carved on a stone plaque with the date 1887 indicates when the house was built, and for whom. Living across the road from the works, the Lumsdens were hands-on employers who enjoyed good relations with their workforce and their many acts of civic generosity were generally appreciated. No longer viable for one family, the mansion has been split into smaller internal units and modern housing has been built in the grounds.

When Thomas Lumsden, who set up the Eden Valley Works, died in 1878 his teenage sons, John and George, were too young to take over, but Mrs Lumsden kept the enterprise going with the assistance of the works manager. This remarkable woman also built the Lumsden Memorial Hall, in 1883, in memory of her husband and later provided it with an endowment of £1,000. The hall, a two storey building with library and reading room on the ground floor and spacious hall upstairs, became a centre of community life. It is seen here just to the right of centre in a picture taken about 1936, looking west along High Street.

Still part of the streetscape, a couple of doors to the west of the Lumsden Hall, this cottage and adjacent shop have been somewhat modified since this picture of them was taken early in the twentieth century.

With the parish church over two miles away in Falkland it is hardly surprising that the first church to be opened in Freuchie was for one of the dissenting churches. It was built in 1796 on the site later used for the Lumsden Memorial Hall and became part of the United Presbyterian Church in 1847. The original building was replaced by a new one, built in Church Street in 1868, and seen here soon after 1900, when it became a United Free Church. After amalgamation with the Church of Scotland in 1929, it was renamed the Scott Memorial Church, but tensions remained between the Freuchie congregations until the 1970s when the old U.P. church was demolished.

Tired of having to trek to the kirk along a dirty, often muddy road, adherents of the established Church of Scotland raised funds for a new church. It was built to the designs of architect Robert Baldie on a site donated by George Johnston of Lathrisk House. Opened in 1876 as a chapel of ease (subordinate to the parish church) it was elevated within a couple of years to being the main church of a quoad sacra parish (an ecclesiastical parish, with no civic responsibilities). After amalgamation of the presbyterian churches in 1929 it became known as the West Church. The interior is seen here about 1902.

Freuchie's war memorial, a simple granite cross, was unveiled in November 1921. It had been erected by builder James Paterson of Newton of Falkland, on a site gifted by Walter Lumsden & Co. of the Eden Valley Works. Major Lumsden presided at the unveiling ceremony which was carried out by Sir Ralph Anstruther, Convenor of Fife County Council. Behind the memorial is Robertson's butchers shop, with his van outside, and the Lomond Hotel (later Lomond Hills Hotel), the oldest part of which dates from 1753.

Originally a mid-nineteenth century subscription school, Freuchie Primary School has been added to and subtracted from so often over the years that it could almost be used for an arithmetic lesson. This picture from 1908 shows the schoolhouse on the left with the dark shadow of the original single storey building clearly visible on the face and gable of the newly completed structure which was also enhanced with the addition of a new porch. The house has since been demolished, but the school is still in use, although its porch has been taken away.

In the early hours of an August morning in 1931 the occupants of the prominent building, just to the right of centre in this picture of Freuchie High Street, were woken by an agitated kitten. Realising that something was wrong the husband pulled on a pair of trousers and dashed downstairs to encounter the choking smoke of a fire that was blazing out of control in the kitchen. He got outside, found a ladder and used it to rescue his wife, three children and two kittens from an upper window. Unable to save the building, fire brigades from Cupar and Auchmuty Mills fought to prevent the blaze from spreading to the neighbouring fruit shop.

The gable of the burned out building can be seen in better times on the left, behind the low pan-tiled roof, in this picture from 1902 looking east along High Street. On the right is Alexander MacKie's shop building, erected in 1900. The parish church is seen through the gap between the Lomond Hills Hotel and a cottage that protruded into the road. It created a narrow, awkward corner that became dangerous as the use of motor vehicles grew, so the County Council bought the cottage and in 1930 knocked it down to widen and improve the road.

Formed in 1908 Freuchie Cricket Club achieved wider fame in 1985 when they beat a team from Surrey, at Lords, to win the National Village Championship. These players from 1922 were also quite successful, winning eleven and drawing three of their 21 fixtures. They are: standing, R. Dewar (Vice-President), E. Croall, A. Simpson, J. Jack (President), R. Duncan (Umpire): sitting, J. Dalrymple, A. Dewar, D. Duncan, J. Lindsay (Captain), J. Baillie, J. Jack jun., D. Low: in front, A. Skinner, A. Wishart (Scorer) and W. Barclay. Two players, G. Allan and R. Bell, were missing on the day.

The thwack of leather on willow would no doubt have been a welcome sound to this team, set up warn Freuchie folk of Second World War air raids. They are, standing, B. Hunter, W. Lindsay, J. Blythe, D. Lumsden and D. Lumsden, and seated, W. Allan, W. Henderson, A. Spence, T. Henderson and J. Allan.

The east end of High Street is seen here looking east to the A92 road in a picture taken about 1905. The Cross Keys, which was later modified with an upper floor and sloping roof, is tucked in discreetly on the right, in front of the large villa facing camera known as Broadmyre. Its name perhaps describes the landscape before it was drained. To its left, behind the horse and cart, is Freuchie Mill Road.

The imposing Freuchie Mill has been converted into flats, the adjacent historic buildings have been restored and a modern housing development has been built alongside. It is neat and tidy compared to the bee hives and unkempt vegetation in front of Freuchie Mill Cottage, the subject of this photograph taken about 1900.

The road north from Kirkcaldy headed through a gap in the hills to Pitillockford. Here the road forked right for Cupar and Dundee, left for Falkland and Perth. These roads were little better than tracks before they were improved after 1790 as turnpike, or toll roads. The toll bar was known as New Inn, after the hostelry that was erected beside it, and its strategic importance was enhanced by the Turnpike Act of 1797 which included a brand new road heading almost due north across the Howe of Fife. Now designated the A92, it was completed to Rathillet by 1802. A kink in its otherwise straight line took it across a new bridge over the Eden at Drumtenant, consigning the earlier Shiells Bridge (below), north of Freuchie, to secondary status. These improved roads encouraged the development of coach services in the early decades of the nineteenth century, and New Inn was well placed to profit from them, but when the railway was driven through the same gap in the hills in the 1840s the coaches lost a lot of trade. The significance of New Inn was further diminished with the ending of the turnpike system in 1878 and this historically important building was demolished in the 1960s to make way for road improvements. The New Inn Roundabout preserves the name.

Semi-detached from the older village of Kingskettle, Kettlebridge developed as a community of weavers. It sat on the north side of the main road, part of the highway that ran between the Tay and Forth ferries. The road was turnpiked in 1790/1791 and became the principal route for some of the early nineteenth century coaches running between the ferry terminals. Their modern equivalents, express buses operating between St Andrews and Glasgow and Edinburgh, roll along the A914, the busy highway that this quiet country road of the 1920s has become.

The railway that spelled the end for the coaches can be seen crossing the bridge at the far end of this early twentieth century view of Back Park. At first glance it looks as if nothing has changed in 100 years, but while the overall character remains, a number of individual houses have been altered.

The parapet of the bridge carrying the main road over Kettle Burn is on the extreme right of this picture looking along North Street. Hidden by the fence and the little hut, the burn flows on, more or less parallel with the street. One of the cottages on the left has a lintel dated 1816 and it is probable that the others were built at much the same time. Skewputs at the ends of the gable copings suggest that originally they were thatched.

The building on the left of this picture incorporates a stone dated 1844 which suggests that these cottages in Mid Street may be a little younger than those of North Street. In the right foreground is the parapet of a neat little 1830s bridge that spans the burn to connect the two streets.

In common with the other towns and villages of the Howe, Kettle's principal manufacturing industry was linen weaving. It was carried out at one principal factory, the Arthurfield Works of D. Beveridge & Co. which was established in 1868. The works, seen here in the early years of the twentieth century, closed in 1930 shortly after the death of the senior partner, Robert Moffat Beveridge.

The architect G. S. Birrell designed Kettle Primary School in 1874 (the date is carved on the front of the building). The plans allowed Kettle School Board to raise a loan, payable over 40 years, and obtain a government grant to pay for the new school. It was opened at the start of the 1875 academic year, although plumbing and painting was still being done and not enough desks had been provided. The picture shows it before the original windows were heightened and more added. The stone pinnacles, some chimneys and the bellcote have also been removed, while the playground has been levelled and hard surfaced.

A major linen factory has grown up and been demolished behind these houses in Rumdewan, but yet there is something serenely unchanging about them. The date, 1879, is displayed on the plaques above the bay windows of the house in the left foreground, and the picture looking towards Kingskettle was taken the 1950s.

Kingskettle's United Presbyterian Church was erected in 1853 and, with its manse alongside, made an imposing sight. Another glorious sight greeted the congregation in mid-January 1875 when a seventeen foot high Christmas tree was set up in the church and decorated with apples, oranges and enough gifts for the 250 children to receive two each. Prince Albert had introduced the Christmas tree to Britain in the 1840s, but it had not been adopted universally when the church held what, for the time, was an unusual celebration. Coinciding with the old Scots Yuletide Festival, it was also a departure for the stern United Presbyterians. A United Free Church after 1900, the building became surplus to requirements when the presbyterian churches reunited in 1929 and it was demolished in the 1960s, although the manse remained.

Erected in 1834, Kettle Parish School was superseded by the new Board school and subsequently became the public hall. At a meeting there in April 1919 the villagers debated what form their war memorial should take and decided to take over the hall, upgrade and extend it, and erect a monument outside. This latter element of the plan was accomplished quickly with a memorial designed by Mr A. F. Balfour Paul and sculpted by Thomas Beattie, both of Edinburgh. Erected by Ladybank builder, D. Nairn, it was unveiled by Major Lawson of Annfield in early April 1920. Two months later a marble shield, presented by the ex-servicemen, was added, and protected by a railing. The public hall was redesignated as the Memorial Hall some time later.

All four pictures on these two pages have one thing in common and show the tower of the parish church standing sentinel over the village. It was built in 1832 to plans prepared by the architect George Angus who must have done well out of the design because it was also used for churches at Kinross and Kincardine-on-Forth. The clock facing camera was installed in December 1928 to commemorate the fifty year ministry of the Reverend Aeneas G. Gordon. A pillar of the local community his retirement coincided with church reunification, after which the building became known as the East Church. The wall in the right foreground of this view of South Street was formerly part of a weaving shed that was incorporated into Kettle Farm.

The original Kingskettle Post Office and shop is seen in this picture looking east along Main Street. The picture is difficult to date, but it was probably taken after 1913 when 73 new gas lamps were erected in the village, although some had been erected on street corners prior to that. The new lamps were paid for by Mr Lawson of Annfield who ceremonially lit the first one outside the public hall. As a token of their gratitude the villagers presented him with a pair of bronze, electric (!) drawing room lamps. The post office has since relocated to South Street and the old premises were transformed into a place of pilgrimage for countless numbers of youngsters when they became the shop and office for the children's entertainers, *The Singing Kettle*. The inset picture shows founders, Artie Trezise (left) and Cilla Fisher, with their colleague Gary Coupland (right) at the start of their 'World Tour Show' in 1993.

In the centre of this mid-twentieth century view of Station Road is the main building of the Kettle Co-operative Society. Predated by earlier societies, the first of which started in 1826, the co-operative was formed in December 1843, one of the earliest in the country. A major retail outlet in the village, its conspicuous presence attracted some unwelcome attention one night in August 1905. Using a plough coulter to force the doors, thieves broke in and rifled through the till, safe and desk drawers, but only got about £20 because the manager had banked the takings the night before. The thieves got the wrong shop because the separate, Kettle Co-operative Baking Society was due to disburse dividend payments the following morning and £600 was lying in their premises. The two societies merged in 1928.

Taken from under the railway bridge, this view of Station Road just catches, on the left hand edge, the balustrade of the beautifully curved stone stair that led up to the station platform. Once a vital part of village life, the station was finally closed in September 1967, having also been shut between January 1917 and February 1919. On the right is a building thought to predate the railway by about a century. At the time the picture was taken early in the twentieth century it was known as the Forester's Inn and run by Mrs Ann Mackenzie. It was later renamed, the Station Inn.

When Archbishop Sharp, an implacable opponent of the Covenanters, was murdered on the road to St Andrews in 1679, one of his assailants was a James Russell of Bankton House. That building no longer exists, but the name is continued by Bankton Park, an enclave of early nineteenth century weavers' cottages on the west side of the railway, while the main part of Kingskettle is to the east. The picture was taken in the 1950s from the railway embankment.

Annfield House sat on high ground above Balmalcolm, with commanding views across the Howe. It was the home of Major Lawson who played a prominent role in the civic affairs of Kettle, but when it ceased to be used as a private house it became a house hotel. Well appointed, with ten rooms and three stars, it was destroyed by fire in November 1980 and the damaged structure was demolished to make it safe.

Balmalcolm developed at much the same time as the turnpike road, the forerunner of the A914, which it straddles. This early twentieth century picture, looking west from the site of the modern bus shelter, shows it as a faintly down-at-heel little village.

Balmalcolm is seen here in a picture taken from Annfield Brae after 1936, the date when the village's Free Church was demolished, following reunification of the three churches in Kettle Parish. The last building on the right was the manse. A fruit and tomato growing business flourished in the first half of the century from the glasshouses on the left. In the 1980s, the Balmalcolm Farm site became the main location used by Kettle Produce to pack vegetables for supermarkets. A major outlet for agricultural produce in North East Fife, the company also operates at Orkie Farm near Freuchie. Just out of picture on the right is Muddy Boots, a farm shop complex developed through the first decade of the twenty-first century.

One industry stood out as being different from all others in the Howe, burning lime to create products for use in construction and agriculture. Huge structures like blast furnaces, over 100 feet tall, stood on the high ground of Cults Hill overlooking Pitlessie. Tubs of crushed limestone were hauled to the top of these on steeply raked metal gantries and their contents were tipped into the kilns where the mineral was subjected to the heat of burning coal gases. Two raw materials were needed, coal and limestone and they both had to be dug from the earth by miners. The last working coal pit in the area was at Rameldry above Kettlebridge, which operated from the early 1890s to the 1920s and is seen here with what was probably the entire workforce. The rickety hutch road, simple little headframe and primitive looking cages suggest an unsophisticated operation.

Limestone miners were not as black as those who worked coal, but they used the same basic equipment like the tally (tallow) lamps pinned to the caps of these Cults men. Such naked flame lamps could be hazardous in gassy coal workings, but not in the inert environment of a stone mine. The limestone beds these men worked at Cults had a calcium carbonate content of 95% and sometimes as high as 99%.

When the Edinburgh and Northern Railway planned a junction and station at the undeveloped spot known as Lady Bog they didn't like the name so they changed it to something that sounded nicer: Ladybank. The line, opened in September 1847, ran north from a ferry terminal at Burntisland to Ladybank where it branched left to Lindores and right to Cupar. These branches were soon extended to Perth, and to Tayport where a ferry took passengers to and from Dundee. Ladybank was thus a key location on the line and increased in importance when it became the eastern terminal of the Fife & Kinross Railway, completed in 1858. Railway workshops were set up in close proximity to the station and Ladybank grew rapidly into a sizeable town. It gained burgh status in 1878. This early twentieth century picture shows the northbound platform, where the main station buildings were erected, perhaps an indication that the company expected most passenger traffic to be going north. The tracks on the left were for trains using the Kinross line.

The heart of the town was grouped around the station as this picture looking toward Commercial Road from Commercial Crescent shows. Facing camera is the former Royal Hotel, one of two such businesses set up in close proximity to the railway. The other, unsurprisingly, was the Railway Hotel. The Royal Hotel has since been replaced by a block of flats.

The station is in the background of this picture taken at the east end of Commercial Road about 1910. Two mounted horsemen watch as a pack of hounds takes a keen interest in something on the footpath: did a fox take a wrong turning? On the wall above the rider on the left is a sign for Dall's cycles. They stocked all the big name bicycles, Raleigh, B.S.A. and Hercules, but also marketed their own Borough Cycles: 'perfect products of practical experience, scientific engineering and technical skill'.

The mounted soldiers on the left of this parade forming up in Commercial Street were from the Fifeshire Royal Field Artillery from Leven. Behind them was the Ladybank Company of the Highland Cyclist Battalion, National Reservists from Ladybank, the Giffordtown and Kingskettle troops of Boy Scouts, and a host of other local groups and schoolchildren preparing to celebrate Empire Day in 1914. Rain began to fall as the parade moved off, but undeterred the marchers and their followers headed for Victoria Park. There they listened to speeches, saluted the flag, applauded patriotic music played by Kettle Band, admired a tableau of Empire and watched a parade of decorated bicycles. When these events were over, a programme of races and sports was held and through it all the rain kept falling.

Railway tracks can be seen in the background of this view of Commercial Crescent taken from the Royal Hotel in 1923. Prominent on the left is the war memorial which was unveiled in November 1921 by Mrs Milbank Leslie Melville of Melville House. The wall behind the memorial was lowered and the ground behind the memorial laid out as the Earl Haig Memorial Garden by ex-servicemen from Ladybank and district, and opened by Countess Haig on a September day in 1931. She performed the ceremony in glorious sunshine which had broken through after the morning's rain. The garden was refurbished in 1993.

The war memorial is on the left and the Royal Hotel on the right of this view looking west along Commercial Road. It is arrow straight, part of a grid system of streets that points to Ladybank's Victorian origins and offers a fascinating contrast with other towns and villages in the Howe that grew over a long time in a random, organic way. The distinctive roofs of the maltings can be seen on the left hand side of the road.

At one time Ladybank had two maltings businesses, one run by Thomas Crichton and another operated by John & James Crichton. They later came together as T. & J. & J. Crichton with extensive premises sandwiched between Commercial Road and the Kinross Railway. The business was taken over in 1935 by Alexander Bonthrone & Sons and then followed the same path as the company's other assets into DCL ownership and eventual closure. Those distinctive roofs were known as Maggies.

Monkstown was originally known as Monksmoss, a name that presumably reflected the boggy ill-drained Howe. Described once as 'an inconsiderable hamlet' it predated Ladybank and appears to have been entirely rebuilt in the 1820s or 1830s, around the time when the village of Kinloch was cleared of its inhabitants. Lowland clearances could be as harsh as Highland clearances, but history has (until recently) ignored them. Many people from that village settled in Monkstown which consisted of six rows of four houses facing a road that in this picture is empty, but in the modern car-dependent world features traffic calming measures. The railway to Kinross ran alongside the road behind the fence on the left. The house on the end of the row on the right has been used as an Episcopal church for many years.

Cyril, who sent this postcard of Church Street to his 'Dear Elsie' in 1917, may have been a soldier stationed at Annsmuir Camp (see page 92). His comments about Ladybank were just a wee bit cynical. Describing the picture as showing 'all there is to see' and the town as a 'noble place', he continued 'you can tell its a gay life here, one round of pleasure from morning until night'. The picture appears to have been taken from the maltings looking north. The tower of the Free Church can be seen in the distance and to the right is the Church of Scotland.

Following the Disruption of 1843 a Free Church for Collessie Parish was built at Giffordtown, but with the arrival of the railway soon afterwards, and the subsequent growth of Ladybank, the majority of the congregation lived a lengthy walk away. This unsatisfactory situation was remedied in 1874 when work began on a new Free Church on a one acre site in Ladybank. The plans, prepared by the architects Peddie & Kinnear of Edinburgh, included a tower, 100 feet high, at one corner and a semicircular apse, seen here. After church union in 1929 the Free Church building was adopted as the parish church.

Ladybank School grew under the auspices of the local school board from a parish school into the substantial building seen here. The picture dates from when the school was expanded with two new classrooms being added along with cooking and laundry rooms, cloakrooms for boys, girls and infants and a headmaster's room which would also be used for school board meetings. The rooms opened into a large, airy hall where, because of bad weather, the opening ceremony for the new extensions was held in April 1911. Mrs Affleck, who performed the ceremony, was presented with a bunch of daffodils by Lizzie Urquhart, the janitor's daughter.

Dating from about 1905, this picture shows Lorne Street looking east toward Melville Road. The cottages on the left have had their chimneys and porches removed, and houses have been built on the vacant ground in the right foreground.

On the right of this view looking west along Kinloch Street is the shop on the Hill Street corner run by James Cunnison. He may have been related to John Cunnison, whose Auchtermuchty shop is shown on page 31, and there also is a strong probability that they both sold the mineral waters made by R. Douglas Ltd., whose Ladybank premises were in Kinloch Street. In the distance is the factory chimney of Wilson and Hill's linen works.

The north end of Hill Street is seen here looking south. The two large blocks of late nineteenth century housing on the left were still relatively new when the picture was taken in 1906. The railings have since been taken away, presumably in the drive for scrap metal during the Second World War. The cottage on the right has been replaced by a modern house.

The distinctive Ladybank water tower was built as part of a new water supply and septic tank sewage system inaugurated in September 1908. Engineers Bruce, Proudfoot and Macrae of Cupar designed the system which drew water from a well and pumped it to the tank on top of the tower. Great care was taken in construction to ensure that surfaces were impervious and that no surface water or pump oil could pollute the supply. The windmill on top was used to drive a pump, but in only its second winter it was damaged by high winds and by March 1910 had been replaced. The supplementary gas engine was superseded by an electric pump in 1928.

Railway sidings and the line to Perth are behind the fence on the right of this early twentieth century picture looking north along Golf Road. The fence, made of old wooden railway sleepers, is typical of a type that was once a universally common feature. With the removal of the sidings the fence has gone and the ground used for modern housing. The older houses on the left have been modified in various ways, but retain the general appearance they had when the picture was taken.

The Fifeshire Auction Company Ltd, formed in November 1899, acquired a site in Golf Street and engaged local contractor Alexander Waddell & Son to erect the necessary buildings. There were stables, byres, a slaughter house and a large and commodious hall for the sale of horses. A dwelling house, on the site when it was acquired, was converted into a licensed bar and refreshment room for customers on sale days. Despite a delay caused by inclement weather the facility was ready for the first sale on 15th February 1900. The company was taken over by Speedie Brothers of Cupar in July 1919.

With the railway between them and the rest of the town, Nairn's Cottages seem a bit cut off, but when this picture was taken in 1905 there was veritable hive of activity going on behind them. A large gate, out of picture on the right, gave access to railway workshops and saw mills. The picture looks out along the Pitlessie road with a horse-drawn travelling shop in the distance.

Originally the Collessie Parish Free Church School, Giffordtown Hall became a social centre for the area and the location of many functions. Typical was one held in April 1918 to provide funds for the wartime Red Cross hospitals at Springfield and Ceres. People donated raffle prizes like a tea cosy, a roast, a steak pie, two laying pullets and a dozen eggs. The livestock auctioneer from Ladybank conducted a sale of these items, the star attraction being a cake made by a woman from the village and decorated with the flags of allied nations. About 100 people attended and after the serious fund-raising, they had tea and danced the night away to the music of Smart and Kemp.

The B937 road was a turnpike road made in the late eighteenth and early nineteenth centuries. Built in a straight line across unenclosed heathland it has become a fast road for modern motor vehicles. Consequently it is easy to miss places along the way, like Giffordtown, on a side track off the main road. The village is seen here in the early years of the twentieth century. Facing camera is a little shop, but at times there was no shopkeeper to run it and villagers had to make long, tiring journeys to get provisions. Motor vehicles and fast roads have eased such hardships.

The Fife Agricultural Society's first show after the First World War was described as a 'Victory Show'. It was held on a beautiful day in June 1919 on a park in front of Ramornie House, home of Colonel Oliver Haig, a nephew of the wartime commander, Field Marshall Earl Haig. The oldest part of Ramornie House dated from 1780, and in its day the estate was famous for its rhododendrons.

The picture left shows the Ramornie Estate gamekeeper, his family, dog and cottage, while to the right, anglers try their luck on the Eden beside the bridge on the Kettle to Ladybank road. These two aspects of country life came together in July 1875 when two

poachers from Dundee were caught beside the river by the Ramornie gamekeeper, Mr McIntosh, and police constable Martin of Kettlebridge. The gentlemen and sportsmen of the area collected money to reward their vigilance.

Annsmuir, to the north of Ladybank, was an excellent place for a military camp. It was flat, close to a railway station, and the sandy, stony ground, which was of little use for agriculture, drained quickly making it ideal for large numbers of men to live under canvas, whatever the weather. Accommodation for horses was provided in four wooden stable buildings. The local volunteer cavalry regiment, the Fife & Forfar Yeomanry, used Annsmuir for their annual camp in the years before the First World War, and during the war other units trained there before heading for the front.

Troops stationed at Annsmuir during the First World War could relax in the recreation hut set up at the camp by the YMCA and manned by volunteers from the local community. There were similar huts at other military training camps and they provided a social refuge for men, far from home, preparing for the hardships and uncertainties of war.

This group of houses has been demolished and replaced by an open green space, that has significantly altered this view of Ladybank Road. All that remains to identify it is the wall on the left and the most distant cottage, which is at the eastern end of School View. The school is behind the bushes on the left.

Known as Hardie's Buildings this fine range of houses stands at the corner of Burnside and High Street which at this point was formerly known as Mercer's Brae. Mary Mercer ran the licensed grocer's shop in the ground floor of the left hand building. In the road a dog, tail alert, eyeballs a cat that is poised to make a dash for safety. A second cat keeps its distance as the early twentieth century's version of a surveillance society watches.

Lister House was built in the late eighteenth century with living quarters on the upper floor and a ground floor workshop. This may originally have been used for weaving, but later became a joiner's shop when the building was acquired by David Garland, the man holding the little girl's hand. The son of a post master he learned his trade during a four year apprenticeship with a John Orford of Kettle Burnside and is thought to have started his own business about 1885.

Pitlessie High Street is seen here looking south to the Cupar Road in the mid-1920s, with a solitary car parked outside the post office. Behind the car is a range of buildings that have since been demolished to create a green space between Couthie's Wynd and the bus shelter on the main road. The cottages on the right have been replaced with modern housing.

Known locally as 'the barns', there were two maltings at Pitlessie operated by Martin Henderson & Company. The one seen here, Pitlessie Maltings, stood alongside the appropriately named Malt Row, the other in Cupar Road was Priestfield Maltings. They had both stopped working some years before their acquisition in 1937 by Alexander Bonthrone & Sons who reconstructed and modernised them, and brought them back into use. A fire in the late 1960s brought work to a halt at Pitlessie Maltings, but malting continued for a while longer at Priestfield. Used for a time as a whisky barrel store, Priestfield Maltings was converted for housing in the mid-1990s.

With the shadow of Pitlessie's Village Inn in the foreground, this picture looks east along Cupar Road about 1905. The prominent building on the right, on the corner of Priestfield Road, has since been demolished and the others to the left have been heavily modified. The two storey building on the left was a linen weaving shop known locally as 'the factory', and one of the single storey buildings next to it was used as a branch of the Kettle Co-operative Society. Round the bend, and thus hidden from view, was the Priestfield Maltings.

There has been a church at Cults for centuries and after the Reformation it came under the patronage of St Andrews University. In 1774 a new minister, the Reverend David Wilkie, was appointed to the parish and he oversaw the building of a new church in 1793 and a new manse three years later.

One stormy evening in November 1926, while the Reverend Porter was visiting a parishioner, the other occupants of Cults Manse heard the family's pet spaniel Tip barking in an agitated way. On investigating, they discovered the minister's study ablaze and despite the strenuous efforts of Cupar Fire Brigade and some volunteers, the building, most of its contents and some valuable church records were destroyed. It was a sad fate for a building with a notable place in Scottish art history. The Reverend Wilkie's son David, born in the old manse in 1785, grew up in the new one. From an early age he showed a remarkable aptitude for art and attended the first permanent art school in Scotland, the Trustee's Academy in Edinburgh. He graduated at the age of nineteen and returned to the manse at Cults where he started to carve out a career that brought a knighthood and a reputation as one the country's finest ever artists.

In 1897 a subscription was started to provide funds for a memorial to Sir David Wilkie. While the money was being raised the committee was offered the Forsyth Hall, the former United Presbyterian Church in Ladybank Road. A quick decision was needed, but the purchase of the hall was not universally welcomed by people who would have preferred a statue or something similar, but the deed was done and the Wilkie Memorial Hall became a focus for community life in the village. It was also used as the site for the Cults Parish War Memorial, erected to the right of the hall entrance and unveiled by Lord Cochrane of Cults in May 1922. The wall behind the three little girls in this picture was lowered to make the war memorial more visible.

One of Wilkie's finest works, *Pitlessie Fair*, painted when he was nineteen years old, has carved the village name permanently into art history. A wonderful image of early nineteenth century village life, it is held by the National Galleries of Scotland. This view, looking north along High Street, contains some elements that can be identified in the picture, notably the small single storey cottage in the distance, on the right hand side of the street projecting beyond the building line, and the two storey house behind it known as Burnbrae. Sir David Wilkie died in 1841 while returning from a sketching tour of the Middle East and was buried at sea.

The mid-eighteenth century Crawford Lodge was extended in the early nineteenth century by Lady Mary Lindsay Crawford, and her architects David Hamilton and J. Gillespie Graham. What they created was Crawford Priory, a highly ornate building with bits that looked like a priory and others that mimicked a castle. Further extensions and embellishments were added about 1871 by the architect William Little working for the Earl of Glasgow.

Once one of the grandest houses in Fife, Crawford Priory saw many distinguished guests, among them, the Right Honourable Joseph Chamberlain MP seen here on 29th October 1901, before giving a speech in Cupar. At the time he was the Government's Colonial Secretary and the principal theme of his address was the South African War, a topic of some concern locally, with the Fife & Forfar Yeomanry actively involved in the fighting. In the picture are seated from the left: Lady Balfour, Mrs Chamberlain and Mrs Blair: standing, Mr Cochrane, Sir John Gilmour, Mr Chamberlain, Mr Anstruther, Miss Marjory Leith, Miss Freda Villiers and Miss Cochrane: and seated on the right are Lady Gertrude Cochrane, the Hon. Henrietta O'Neill and the Hon. Mary Bruce.

Russell Mills was being worked by operating tenants in 1856 when the owner, William Moon of Edenfield, sold it to Smith, Laing & Company. With experience in the Dundee jute industry they set about making the mills into a major employer in the Springfield area, opening new capacity about 1876. Smith, Laing became a private limited company in 1920 with G. B. Smith as chairman, but in 1935, following his death three years earlier, the mills were sold and the machinery dismantled.

The Lunacy (Scotland) Act of 1857 established a General Board of Commissioners in Lunacy to regulate provision for the mentally ill. District boards were also set up including one for Fife and Kinross, which moved with some speed to build a new asylum near Springfield for those people described in the act as pauper lunatics. It had accommodation for 223 patients and was opened without any ceremony in July 1866. The overall site extended to 57 acres, ideal for activities like farming and gardening that were regarded at the time as ideal therapy. Proximity to the railway line was also a key element in selecting the site so that supplies could be delivered and people could visit. Since its opening the institution has been altered in many ways, including a name change to Stratheden Hospital.

It's not a frequent event but, over fifty years after the Beeching cuts, trains stop at Springfield's little station, just out of picture, round the corner on the left. In the centre of this view of the southern end of Station Road are the New Cottages which, although heavily altered, remain in place. The tenement buildings to left and right have all disappeared, the ones on the left having been replaced by the Crawford Park housing development.

Looking south along Station Road, this view from 1913 is still recognisable despite a number of changes and some blocks of council housing having been built on the left. What has noticeably changed about this picture and the one above is the string of traffic calming measures from one end of the village to the other. These, and the volume of traffic that made them a necessity, mean that any attempt to position a horse-hauled vehicle in the middle of the road for a photograph would be unwise.

Lord Cochrane was ill, so it was Lady Cochrane who read his prepared speech and unveiled Springfield War Memorial on 8th January 1922. The simple Aberdeen granite Celtic cross had been erected by two contractors from Cupar, builders R. G. Findlay, and the Central Garage and Engineering Works, who made the railings. The enclosed ground was laid out with gravel and shrubs by the gardener from Russell Mills.

David Maitland-Makgill Crichton of Nether Rankeillour House was a significant figure in the development of Springfield, so the spelling of Makgill Row suggests that these houses may have a link to the estate, or were built on ground feued from it. The picture shows the row about 1905.

The Springfield Branch of the Cupar and District Co-operative Society was destroyed by fire in February 1915. Cupar Fire Brigade arrived almost two hours after the fire was first noticed, so there was nothing left to save, but the crew ran their hoses to the old quarry half a mile away and broke the ice to get water. They damped down the smouldering remains and made sure that neighbouring properties were safe. Mice nibbling at matches in the store room were thought to have been the cause of the blaze.

Two days after the fire a temporary store was opened in Main Street and, to the Co-op's delight, it showed an increase in takings from the old store, despite being in a less favoured location. Not satisfied with that, the Co-op set about rebuilding the old shop to plans drawn up the architect H. A. Newman of Cupar. The principal alterations were larger windows and a heightened roof which created more storage space. The reinstated premises were opened in mid-September by Society President William N. Mitchell and, as soon as he had performed the ceremony, customers rushed in, vying with each other to be first to use the new store.

Fernie & Finlay of Cupar were the main building contractors engaged to enlarge the former Free Church school building in Springfield. While doing preparatory work in July 1874 they removed the old foundation stone and found under it a bottle that had been placed there during the earlier construction. It contained some silver coins, a bill of sale for timber, a copy of the *Fife Herald* from 4th September 1828 and a note stating that the stone had been laid on 6th September by David Maitland Makgill Crichton of Nether Rankeillour. Springfield School has seen a few more changes since then.

This view looking north along Main Street was taken in the mid-1920s. Since then most of the houses on the left have been replaced by modern single storey dwellings. Some buildings on the right have also been altered, but again the most obvious change is that the road is no longer the empty track seen here, but one heavily used by motor vehicles negotiating an obstacle course of traffic calming measures.

The *Oxford Dictionary* defines a hamlet as 'a small village, especially one without a church', so that rules out the Bow of Fife because if there is one thing the tiny village had, it was a church. The foundation stone was laid in 1853 for the Monimail Free Church, built for a congregation that had split from Monimail Church as a result of the Disruption. The church was rebuilt in 1898 by Sir Michael Nairn of Rankeillour and the distinctive spire was also added at that time. Further alterations, including the installation of a pipe organ, were made by Sir Michael in 1912. The first minister, the Reverend James Brodie, built the manse out of his own funds.

At the start of the nineteenth century, when the road running north across the Howe to the Tay was upgraded to turnpike status, a toll bar was set up at Letham. It had been disused for some time when this picture was taken early in the twentieth century, although the toll cottage remained. The road, seen here as a narrow country track has, almost unbelievably, become the wide, fast, A92 road and a somewhat hazardous place for chickens. At the cross roads just beyond the cottage, the road to the right goes to Bow of Fife, to the left is Letham.

The road from Letham Toll runs up the hill to the village, with this impressive row of cottages facing south-west to the Lomond Hills. Restoration as modern dwellings has given them a life beyond the village-based activities of their early occupations, one of which was the local saddler R. Storrar whose painted sign has been retained on the face of a cottage a couple down from the top. It was later used as Storrar's Emporium and the Letham Post Office, before that moved to School Brae.

Tom Paxton, stately and erect,
Has lang since won oor best respect . . .
Unknown frae Fife to oor auld Toon,
He came wi' less than hauf-a-croon . . .

Sir Thomas Paxton Bt was born in Collessie in 1860 and brought up in this cottage in School Brae, Letham. Apprenticed as a joiner, he left Letham and moved to Glasgow where he went into commerce, eventually setting up a large emporium in the Gorbals known as the Adelphi Stores. Turning to politics he was elected first to Govan Parish Council and then the town council of Glasgow where his record as a civic leader, from humble origins, was put to verse (above) in 1910. He had made a little more than 'hauf-a-croon' by the time he was elected Lord Provost of the city in November 1920, a post he held for three years. Amongst many honours, he was awarded an Honorary Doctorate of Laws by St Andrews University in 1922 and became a Baronet in the New Year Honours List in 1923.

The photographer who took this picture looking down School Brae, Letham, has chosen neither a bright summer's day, nor a crisp midwinter scene, but has instead gone for bare trees, soft shadows and hazy light. It has made for a superb image of the Fife countryside and, with a little group of children sitting beside the road, it is a scene redolent of a painting by Dundee artist James McIntosh Patrick. Just beyond the small cottage on the left is the blank back wall of a doocot, a structure intended to provide a nesting place for pigeons which could fatten themselves on the pickings of the countryside before forming the basis of a meal to fatten their owners. More of these structures have survived in Fife than elsewhere in Scotland: the one in the picture is of a type known as a lectern doocot.

The 'Village Green', the title of this picture from the 1920s, is seen here looking west from Letham Farm. The late eighteenth century farmhouse of Letham Lands is on the extreme right. In common with most of these buildings it has been updated, and the one seen through the gap just to the right of centre has gone, but despite the changes the village has retained its essential character.

These children in Monimail Road, Letham, are playing a game widely known as *London Bridge* in which two children create a bridge with their arms while the others hold on to each other and run through it, dreading the moment when the bridge falls and catches one of them. A Scottish version of the game was recorded in 1901 which, instead of London Bridge, started with the words *Broken bridges falling down, falling down, falling down; Broken bridges falling down, my fair ladies*. Intriguingly this picture by local photographer R. J. P. Spence is entitled *Broken Bridge*, so perhaps this little bit of Scottish social history remained strong in North East Fife while weakening elsewhere. The children's clothing is also interesting with the girl in the striped dress wearing a hat on her head, but nothing on her feet.

Monimail's church connections go back over eight centuries, to when it became the private estate of the Bishops (and in 1471 the Archbishops) of St Andrews. A tower, part of their former residence, stands in the grounds of Melville House and a fragment of the fifteenth century church remains in the kirkyard. The post-Reformation parish church was erected in the 1790s, with the tower being added in 1811. Somewhat remote in a relatively thinly populated parish, its wonderfully Spartan old Scots kirk interior was still intact at the start of the twenty-first century.

Letham and Monimail were estate villages that grew under the patronage of the church and then the landed lairds of Melville. By the early nineteenth century a high percentage of residents worked as hand loom weavers, but with the growth of the power loom factories the population declined. People who worked at other things lost their customers when the weavers left and they also drifted away until the only craftsman left was the blacksmith working at his smithy down in the den.

Melville House is one of Fife's and Scotland's grandest mansions. Erected between 1697 and 1703, it was designed by the architect James Smith who had been tutored by Sir William Bruce and succeeded him as Overseer of the Royal Works in Scotland. With little work being required by the Crown, this was a largely symbolic role, but the honour of holding such a post was a recognition that Smith was regarded as the foremost Scottish architect of his time.

The main, tree-lined approach to Melville House left the public road at gates flanked by two widely spaced lodges. In attempting to include the two buildings in this picture the photographer has filled the frame with the crossroads that grew in notoriety along with the rise in the use of motor vehicles. After numerous accidents the crossroads was replaced by a roundabout, named after the lodges that were removed to make way for it.

The building with its gable facing camera on the right was built as a coaching inn just before the Battle of Trafalgar in 1805, and named after it. The name was also adopted for the cluster of buildings around the inn. This picture taken in Edwardian times, shows the road junction as it was before a spate of traffic accidents led to the five roads at the intersection being offset. The inn has since been demolished, but a small commemorative plaque was erected on the site in 2005.

The main road at Trafalgar, the A91, was an old road that ran between St Andrews and Stirling, crossing the Great North Road at the county border. With Fife a peninsula it was a vital route in and out of the north side of the county, and it was turnpiked after 1790, but in the 1960s developments elsewhere began to have a big impact on it. Glasgow, Scotland's industrial and economic powerhouse, began to dwindle while, at the same time, the Forth Road Bridge, the M90 and the dual carriageway A92 shifted Fife's focus south to a resurgent Edinburgh. The Tay Bridge ended the disadvantages of living on a peninsula and vehicle movements switched to a north-south direction instead of east-west. In the space of only a few decades the A91 had lost its strategic importance, and much of its traffic.

A roughish road surface, slower vehicles and a more leisurely pace to life meant that people approaching Collessie from Monimail would have time to savour this view. It contained many of the elements that characterised the Howe: the distant Lomond Hills, the church tower and the rich farmland bounded by dykes and hedges. Half-hidden behind the hedge on the left is the Victory Hall dated 1923. The people of the scattered rural parish were torn as to how best to commemorate their war dead, so while the hall was built at Collessie, the memorial was erected beside Giffordtown Hall.

Once an essential part of village life, the post office has disappeared from many places like Collessie and only the presence of a post box or telephone kiosk remains as a clue to where they once were, and these facilities are under threat from mobile phones and e-mails. When this picture of the post office and general store was taken in the 1920s, it was run by an M. Coupar. On the right is the end of one of the cottages that were combined as Rose Cottage, one of the picturesque thatched cottages that have given the village its distinctive character.